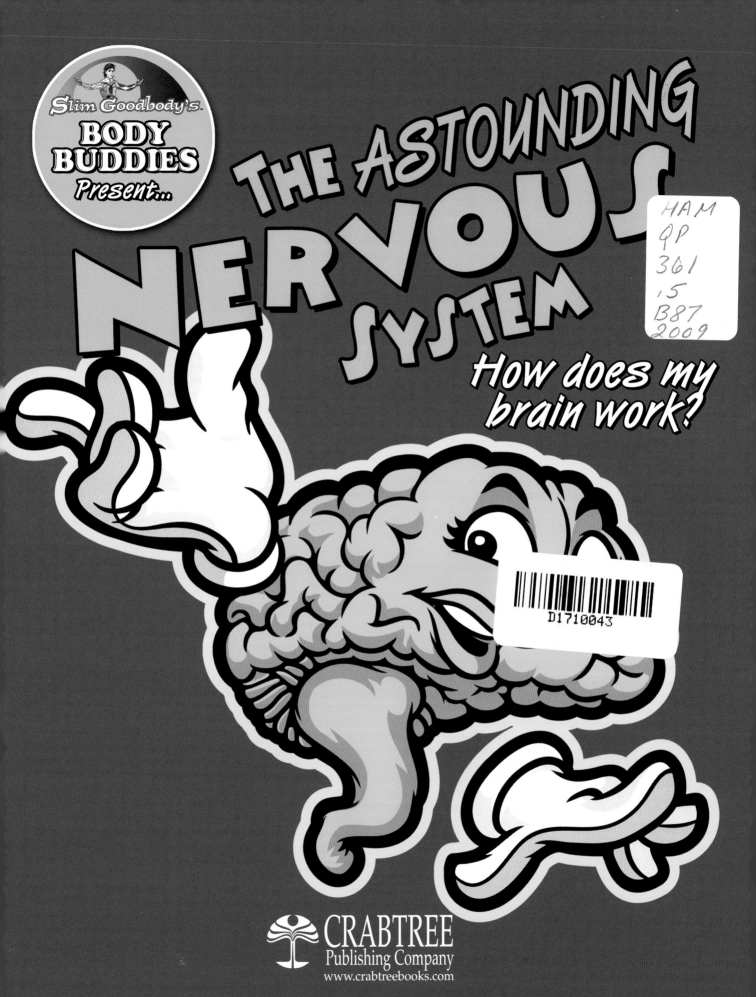

Slim Goodbody's™
BODY BUDDIES
Present...

THE ASTOUNDING
NERVOUS
SYSTEM

How does my brain work?

CRABTREE
Publishing Company
www.crabtreebooks.com

Crabtree Publishing Company
www.crabtreebooks.com

Series Development, Writing, and Packaging:
John Burstein Slim Goodbody Corp.

Medical Reviewer:
Christine S. Burstein, RN, MSN, FNP

Designer: Tammy West, Westgraphix

Project coordinator: Robert Walker

Editors: Mark Sachner, Water Buffalo Books
Molly Aloian

Proofreader: Adrianna Morganelli

Print and production coordinator: Katherine Berti

Prepress technicians:
Rosie Gowsell, Ken Wright

Picture credits:
© istockphoto: cover, p. 9a, 13, 15a, 25b, 26, 27c
© Shutterstock: p. 16
© Slim Goodbody: p. 9b, 11, 12, 15b, 17, 21,
22, 23, 24, 25a

Cognos Character Design and Illustration:
Mike Ray, Ink Tycoon

Medical Illustrations: Colette Sands,
Render Ranch, and Mike Ray

"Slim Goodbody," "Cognos," and Render Ranch
illustrations, copyright © Slim Goodbody

Library and Archives Canada Cataloguing in Publication

Burstein, John
The astounding nervous system : how does my brain work?
/ John Burstein.

(Slim Goodbody's body buddies)
Includes index.
ISBN 978-0-7787-4414-6 (bound).--ISBN 978-0-7787-4428-3 (pbk.)

1. Nervous system--Juvenile literature. I. Title.
II. Series: Burstein, John . Slim Goodbody's body buddies.

QP361.5.B87 2009   j612.8   C2008-907867-5

Library of Congress Cataloging-in-Publication Data

Burstein, John.
The astounding nervous system : how does my brain work?
/ John Burstein.
p. cm. -- (Slim Goodbody's body buddies)
Includes index.
ISBN 978-0-7787-4428-3 (pbk. : alk. paper) -- ISBN 978-0-7787-4414-6
(reinforced library binding : alk. paper)
1. Nervous system--Juvenile literature. 2. Brain--Juvenile literature.
I. Title. II. Series.

QP361.5.B87 2009
612.8--dc22

2008052371

Crabtree Publishing Company
www.crabtreebooks.com   1-800-387-7650

Printed in the U.S.A./092015/CG20150812

Published in Canada
Crabtree Publishing
616 Welland Ave.
St. Catharines, Ontario
L2M 5V6

Published in the United States
Crabtree Publishing
PMB 59051
350 Fifth Avenue, 59th Floor
New York, New York 10118

Published in the United Kingdom
Crabtree Publishing
Maritime House
Basin Road North, Hove
BN41 1WR

Published in Australia
Crabtree Publishing
3 Charles Street
Coburg North
VIC, 3058

About the Author
John Burstein (also known as Slim Goodbody) has been entertaining and educating children for over thirty years. His programs have been broadcast on CBS, PBS, Nickelodeon, USA, and Discovery. He has won numerous awards including the Parent's Choice Award and the President's Council's Fitness Leader Award. Currently, Mr. Burstein tours the country with his multimedia live show "Bodyology." For more information, please visit slimgoodbody.com.

CONTENTS

MEET THE BODY BUDDIES 4

THE LEADER OF THE BAND 6

BUSY, BUSY, BUSY 8

HALF AND HALF 10

TEAMWORK 12

BODY BASICS 14

GET THE MESSAGE! 16

THE NERVOUS SYSTEM 18

SENSATIONAL SENSES 20

MAKING SENSE OF SENSES 22

THE LOVE OF LEARNING 24

BRAIN BELIEFS 26

FABULOUS PHRASES 28

AMAZING FACTS ABOUT YOUR NERVOUS SYSTEM 29

GLOSSARY 30

FOR MORE INFORMATION 31

INDEX 32

Words in **bold** are defined in the glossary on page 30.

MEET THE BODY BUDDIES

I am very happy that you are reading this book. It means that you want to learn about your body!

I believe that the more you know about how your body works, the prouder you will feel.

I believe that the prouder you feel, the more you will do to take care of yourself.

I believe that the more you do to take care of yourself, the happier and healthier you will be.

To provide you with the very best information about how your body works, I have put together a team of good friends. I call them my Body Buddies, and I hope they will become your Body Buddies, too!

Let me introduce them to you:

- **HUFF AND PUFF** will guide you through the lungs and the respiratory system.

- **TICKER** will lead you on a journey to explore the heart and circulatory system.

- **COGNOS** will explain how the brain and nervous system work.

- **SQUIRT** will let you in on the secrets of tiny glands that do big jobs.

- **FLEX AND STRUT** will walk you through the workings of your bones and muscles.

- **GURGLE** will give you a tour of the stomach and digestive system.

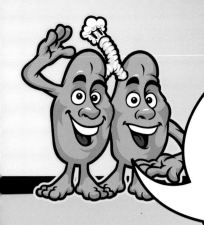

HUFF & PUFF Say...
YOUR RESPIRATORY SYSTEM IS MADE UP OF YOUR LUNGS, ALL THE AIRWAYS CONNECTED WITH THEM, AND THE MUSCLES THAT HELP YOU BREATHE.

TICKER Says...
YOUR CIRCULATORY SYSTEM IS MADE UP OF YOUR HEART, WHICH PUMPS YOUR BLOOD, AND THE TUBES, CALLED BLOOD VESSELS, THROUGH WHICH YOUR BLOOD FLOWS.

COGNOS Says...
YOUR NERVOUS SYSTEM IS MADE UP OF YOUR BRAIN, SPINAL CORD, AND ALL THE NERVES THAT RUN THROUGHOUT YOUR BODY.

SQUIRT Says...
YOUR ENDOCRINE SYSTEM IS MADE UP OF MANY DIFFERENT GLANDS THAT PRODUCE SUBSTANCES TO HELP YOUR BODY WORK RIGHT.

GURGLE Says...
YOUR DIGESTIVE SYSTEM HELPS TURN THE FOOD YOU EAT INTO ENERGY. IT INCLUDES YOUR STOMACH, LIVER, AND INTESTINES.

FLEX & STRUT Say...
YOUR MUSCULAR SYSTEM IS MADE UP OF MUSCLES THAT HELP YOUR BODY MOVE. THE SKELETAL SYSTEM IS MADE UP OF THE BONES THAT HOLD YOUR BODY UP.

THE LEADER OF THE BAND

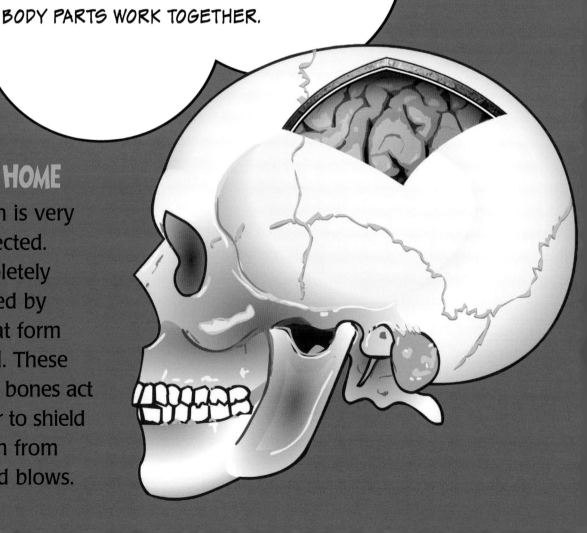

HELLO.
MY NAME IS COGNOS.

I AM A BRAIN. PEOPLE SAY I AM THE BOSS OF THE BODY. ACTUALLY, I AM MORE LIKE THE LEADER OF A BAND. THE HUMAN BODY HAS TRILLIONS OF CELLS AND DOZENS OF BODY PARTS.
I MAKE SURE ALL OF THE CELLS AND BODY PARTS WORK TOGETHER.

A BONE HOME

Your brain is very well protected. It is completely surrounded by bones that form your skull. These hard skull bones act like armor to shield your brain from bangs and blows.

HUFF &
PUFF say...
LUNGS ARE ALSO
PROTECTED BY BONES.
THE **RIB CAGE**
KEEPS US SAFE.

LAYERS OF LINING

Between your hard skull bones and
your soft brain, there are three layers
of material called **meninges**. Meninges
give your brain extra protection:

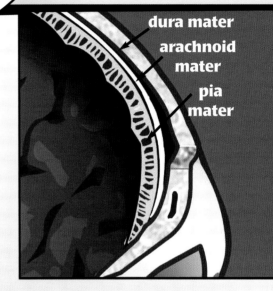

dura mater
arachnoid mater
pia mater

1. The dura mater lines the inside of the skull.

2. The pia mater covers the brain itself.

3. The arachnoid mater lies between the
dura mater and the pia mater.

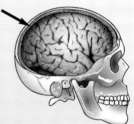

meninges

Between the arachnoid mater and the pia mater is a
clear fluid. It is called cerebrospinal fluid. This fluid adds
an extra cushion of protection to keep your brain safe.

BE A SCIENTIST

Here is an experiment to help you
understand how fluids (like your
cerebrospinal fluid) can cushion falls.

**Here is what you
will need:**
• One empty bucket
• Two eggs
• Water

Directions:

1. Hold the first egg about one foot (0.3 m)
above the bucket and let go.

2. Clean the bucket.

3. Fill the bucket with water.

4. Hold the second egg about one foot
(0.3 m) above the bucket and let go.

What happens each time you let an egg
drop? Does water cushion the fall?

BUSY, BUSY, BUSY

EVERY SINGLE MOMENT OF EVERY SINGLE DAY, I AM BUSY. I THINK, I PLAN, I DECIDE, I REMEMBER, AND I DREAM. I KEEP A CONSTANT CHECK ON THE HEART, THE LUNGS, THE STOMACH, AND ALL THE OTHER ORGANS. I NEVER TAKE TIME OFF.

DIFFERENT PARTS

Your brain is divided into different parts. Three of the most important parts are the cerebrum, the cerebellum, and the brain stem. Each part has different responsibilities.

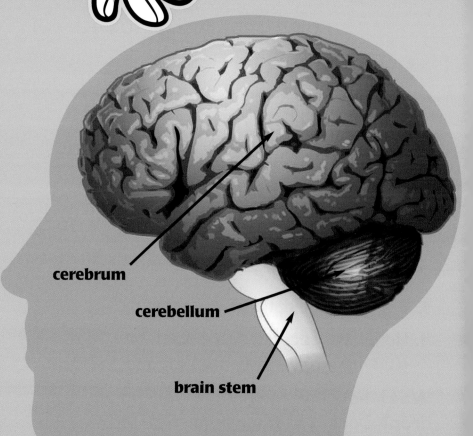

cerebrum

cerebellum

brain stem

FLEX & STRUT say...

EVEN WHILE YOU SLEEP, YOUR BRAIN SENDS MESSAGES THROUGH **NERVES** TO TELL US TO TURN YOU OVER.

1. WHAT IS THE CAPITAL OF ENGLAND?

2. HOW MANY MONTHS ARE IN TWO YEARS?

3. WHAT ARE FIVE WORDS THAT RHYME WITH "HAT"?

THE CEREBRUM

The cerebrum is more than twice the size of any of the other parts of your brain. The cerebrum is responsible for thinking, planning, imagining, dreaming, and making decisions. You are using your cerebrum right now to read and understand this book. You also use your cerebrum to answer questions.

BARK, BARK

The outer surface of the cerebrum is called the cerebral cortex. The word "cortex" comes from a Latin word that means "bark." The cortex covers the brain, just as bark covers the outside of a tree.

cerebral cortex

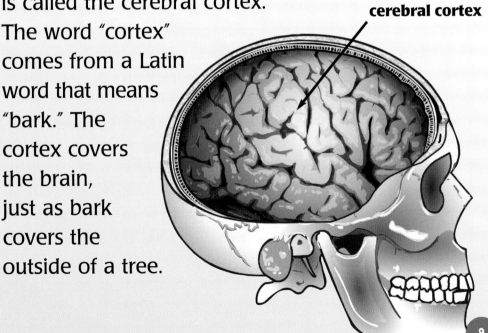

HALF AND HALF

WHEN YOU LOOK AT THE CEREBRUM, YOU WILL SEE IT IS DIVIDED IN HALF. EACH HALF IS CALLED A **HEMISPHERE**. I HAVE A LEFT HEMISPHERE AND A RIGHT HEMISPHERE.

MATH AND MUSIC

The two hemispheres of your cerebrum work together, but each one is better at some kinds of thinking. The left hemisphere is better at solving math problems and reading directions. The right hemisphere is better at making art and playing music. The hemispheres are connected by a thick band of nerves called the corpus callosum.

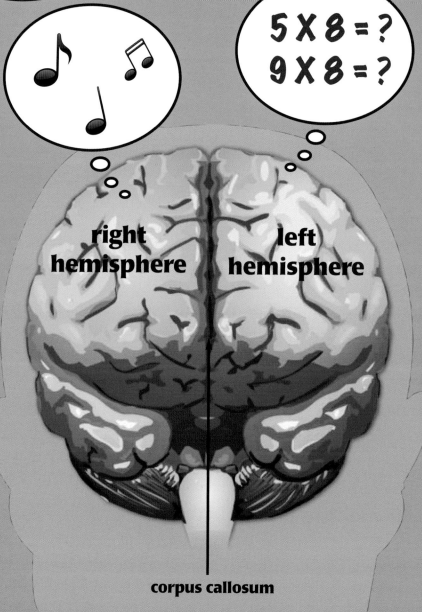

5 X 8 = ?
9 X 8 = ?

right hemisphere

left hemisphere

corpus callosum

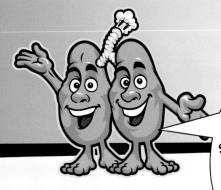

HUFF &
PUFF say...
YOUR BRAIN IS NOT THE
ONLY ORGAN THAT HAS
SECTIONS CALLED **LOBES**.
YOUR LUNGS ALSO HAVE
LOBES – FIVE OF THEM.

A LOT OF LOBES

Each hemisphere is divided into four different sections. These sections are called **lobes**. Lobes have different responsibilities:

1. The frontal lobes are responsible for helping you solve problems.

2. The temporal lobes are responsible for helping you hear and remember.

3. The occipital lobes are responsible for helping you understand what you see.

4. The parietal lobes are responsible for helping you understand what you touch.

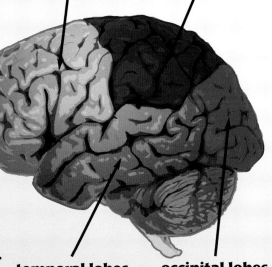

frontal lobes   **parietal lobes**

temporal lobes   **occipital lobes**

gyri

sulci

WHY WRINKLES?

Your cortex is not smooth and flat. It has a lot of bulges and grooves that make it look very wrinkly. The bulges are called **gyri**. The grooves are called **sulci**. Wrinkles allow more material to fit inside a small space.

For example, if you took a big piece of paper and crumpled it up into a wrinkly ball, it would fit inside a juice glass. If you could smooth out the folds and wrinkles of the cortex, it would cover an area about the size of a full page of a newspaper!

TEAMWORK

I DO NOT SPEND ALL MY TIME THINKING. I ALSO CONTROL THE MOVEMENT OF THE MUSCLES. THERE ARE MORE THAN 600 DIFFERENT MUSCLES IN THE BODY. I MAKE SURE THEY ALL WORK TOGETHER AND THAT THE RIGHT MUSCLE MAKES THE RIGHT MOVE AT JUST THE RIGHT TIME! THE PART I USE FOR THIS JOB IS THE CEREBELLUM.

IN BACK

Your cerebellum is located below the back part of your cerebrum. The cerebellum is only about one-tenth the size of your cerebrum, but do not let the small size fool you. Controlling muscle movement is a very big job.

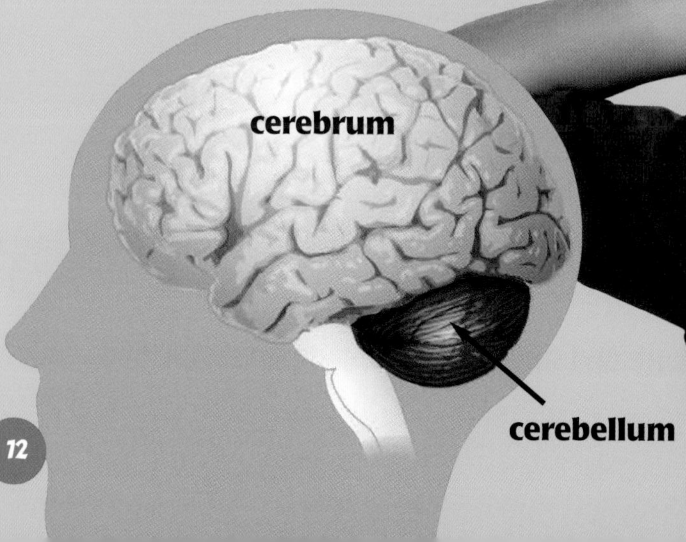

cerebrum

cerebellum

COGNOS says...
EVERY MOVE YOU MAKE REQUIRES DIFFERENT GROUPS OF MUSCLES TO WORK TOGETHER. WHEN MUSCLES WORK TOGETHER, IT IS CALLED **COORDINATION.**

SIDE BY SIDE

Just like your cerebrum, your cerebellum is divided into two hemispheres. The right hemisphere coordinates movement on the left side of your body. The left hemisphere coordinates movement on the right side of your body.

left hemisphere   **right hemisphere**

BE A SCIENTIST

In this experiment you will demonstrate how coordination works.

Directions:

1. Touch the tip of your right **index finger** to the tip of your nose.

2. Touch the tip of your left index finger to the tip of your nose.

Here is what you will need:
- Your finger
- Your nose

If your cerebellum was not working right, the touching motions would be very jerky. These were simple movements, and yet they required the coordination of muscles in your back, shoulders, arms, hands, and eyes.
Think about all the coordination it takes to do gymnastics, play the piano, or jump rope.

BODY BASICS

WHILE MY CEREBRUM AND CEREBELLUM ARE BUSY DOING THEIR JOBS, I MUST ALSO KEEP A CHECK ON OTHER IMPORTANT THINGS.

IS THE HEART BEATING FAST ENOUGH?

IS FOOD MOVING WELL THROUGH THE INTESTINES?

IS THERE ENOUGH OXYGEN IN THE BLOOD?

THESE ARE SOME OF THE BASIC THINGS THAT MUST HAPPEN TO KEEP THE BODY ALIVE. CHECKING UP ON THESE BASICS IS THE JOB OF MY BRAIN STEM.

LOW DOWN

The brain stem is the lowest part of your brain. The brain stem makes sure that your involuntary muscles are doing their jobs well. Involuntary muscles are the ones that work without you thinking about them. Your heart is an involuntary muscle and involuntary muscles push food through the digestive system.

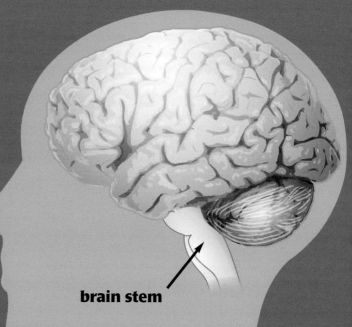

brain stem

14

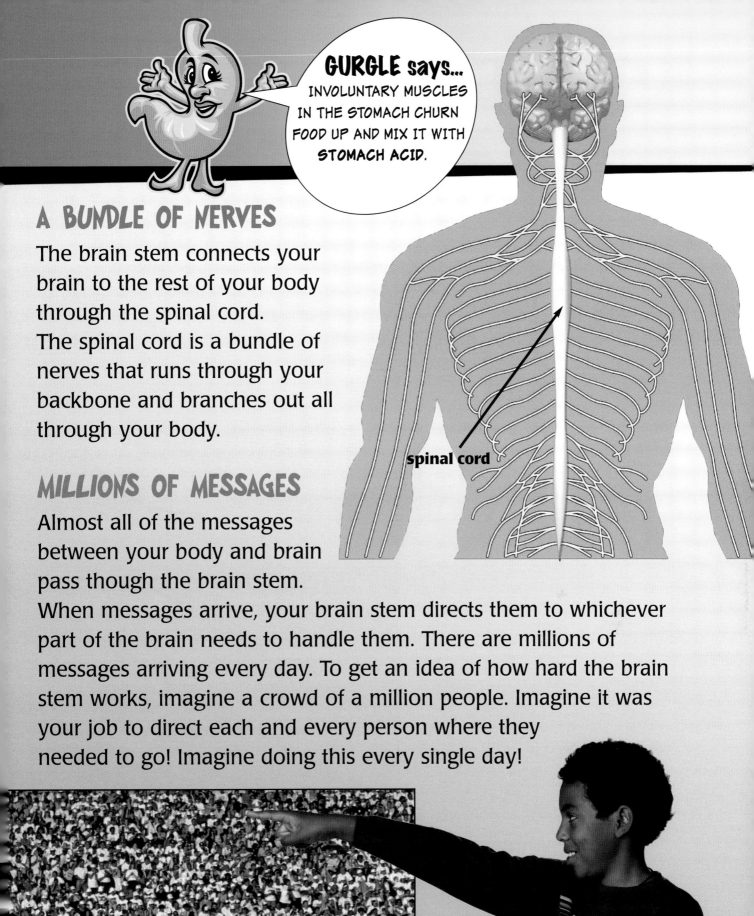

GURGLE says...
INVOLUNTARY MUSCLES IN THE STOMACH CHURN FOOD UP AND MIX IT WITH STOMACH ACID.

A BUNDLE OF NERVES

The brain stem connects your brain to the rest of your body through the spinal cord. The spinal cord is a bundle of nerves that runs through your backbone and branches out all through your body.

spinal cord

MILLIONS OF MESSAGES

Almost all of the messages between your body and brain pass though the brain stem. When messages arrive, your brain stem directs them to whichever part of the brain needs to handle them. There are millions of messages arriving every day. To get an idea of how hard the brain stem works, imagine a crowd of a million people. Imagine it was your job to direct each and every person where they needed to go! Imagine doing this every single day!

GET THE MESSAGE!

IF I WANT TO CONTACT THE TOES, I DO NOT SEND THEM A TEXT MESSAGE. IF THE TOES WANT TO CONTACT ME, THEY DO NOT CALL ME UP ON THE TELEPHONE. MESSAGES PASS ALONG A WONDERFUL COMMUNICATION SYSTEM MADE UP OF BILLIONS OF NERVE CELLS.

A SPECIAL NAME

Nerve cells have a special name. They are called neurons. A neuron has three main parts:

1. A cell body
2. A long thin branch called the axon.
3. Several short branches called dendrites

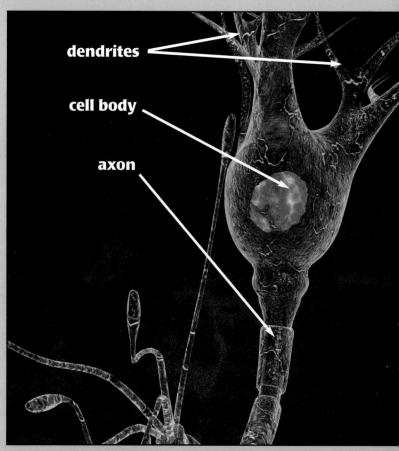

dendrites

cell body

axon

TICKER says...
YOU HAVE TWO KINDS OF NEURONS. SENSORY NEURONS CARRY MESSAGES FROM THE BODY TO THE BRAIN. MOTOR NEURONS SEND MESSAGES FROM THE BRAIN BACK TO THE BODY.

A LITTLE ELECTRICITY

Neurons send tiny electric signals to carry information. Here is how:

1. The electrical signal travels through the neuron and down its axon.

2. When the signal reaches the end of the axon, it jumps across a tiny gap to the next neuron. This tiny gap between one neuron and the next is called a synapse.

3. On the other side of the synapse, the electrical signal reaches one of the dendrites in the next neuron. The signal moves up the dendrite and into the axon.

4. At the end of the axon, the signal jumps to the next dendrite in line.

5. On and on it goes, from one neuron to the next in a long chain to or from the brain.

synapse

axon

dendrites

electrical signal

cell body

synapse

BE A SCIENTIST

In this experiment you will create a model of a neuron.

Here is what you will need:
• Your arm and hand

Directions:
Hold out your arm and spread your fingers. In this model your hand is the "cell body." Your fingers are the "dendrites" bringing information to the cell body. Your arm is the "axon" taking information away from the cell body.

THE NERVOUS SYSTEM

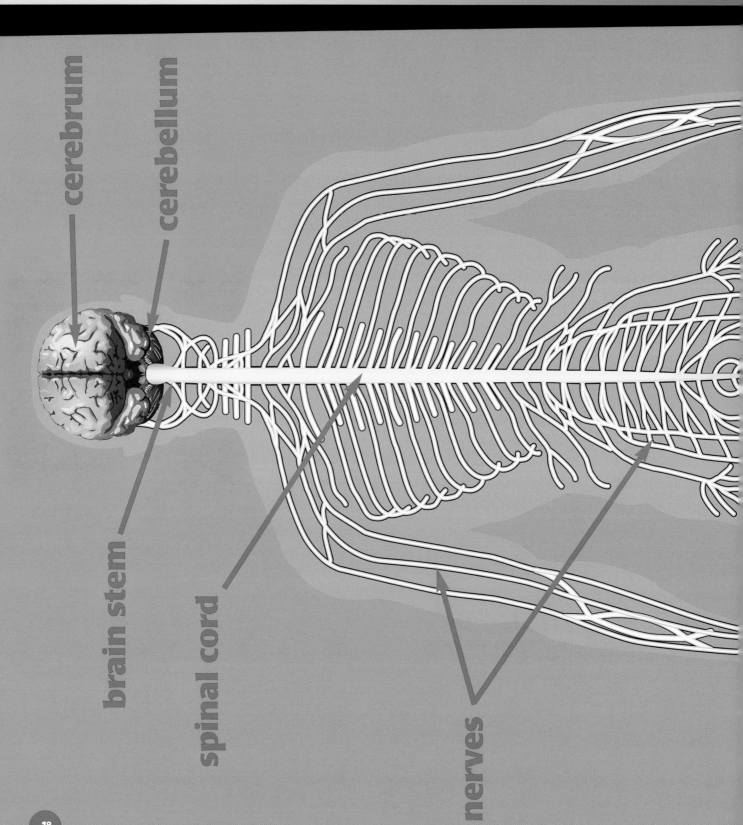

cerebrum

cerebellum

brain stem

spinal cord

nerves

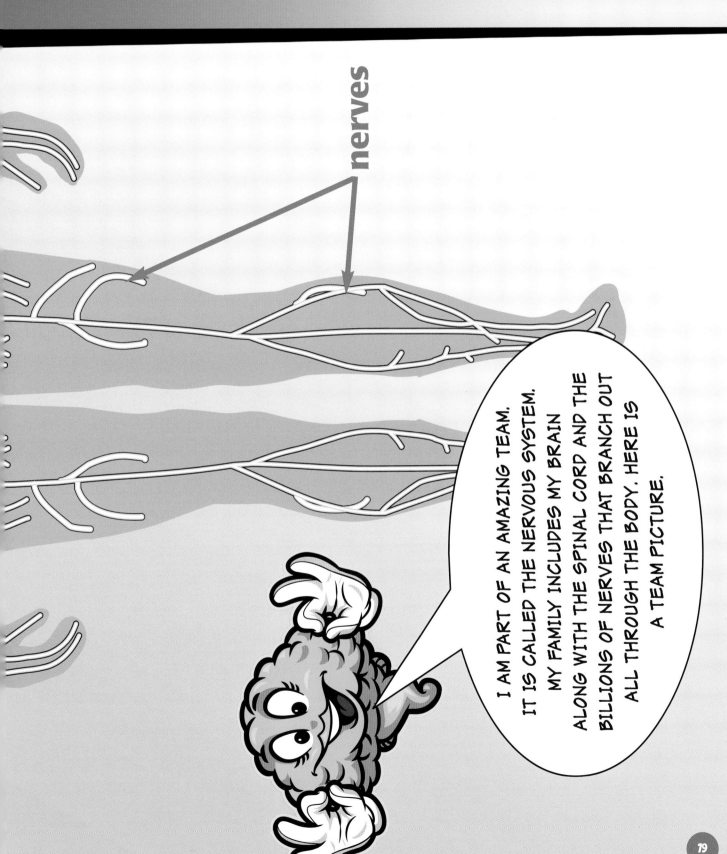

nerves

I AM PART OF AN AMAZING TEAM. IT IS CALLED THE NERVOUS SYSTEM. MY FAMILY INCLUDES MY BRAIN ALONG WITH THE SPINAL CORD AND THE BILLIONS OF NERVES THAT BRANCH OUT ALL THROUGH THE BODY. HERE IS A TEAM PICTURE.

SENSATIONAL SENSES

THE FIVE SENSES HELP ME UNDERSTAND WHAT IS AROUND ME. INFORMATION IS SENT TO ME BY NEURONS IN THE EYES, EARS, NOSE, MOUTH, AND SKIN. I USE THIS INFORMATION TO TAKE CARE OF THE BODY.

SENSE MAP

Each of your five senses sends messages to a different area in the cerebrum.

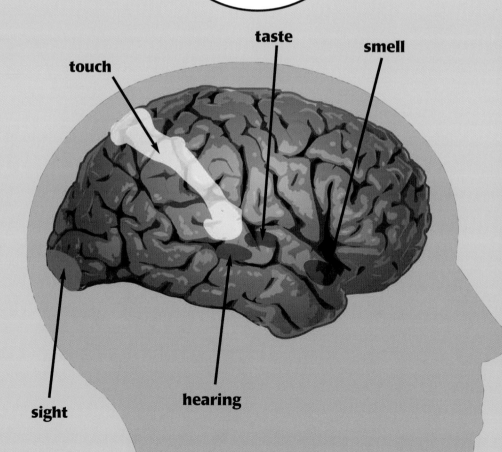

touch

taste

smell

sight

hearing

Your skin contains millions of neurons. They send messages to your brain about what you touch. Most of these neurons are located in the fingers, tongue, and lips.

You have about 100 million neurons at the back of your eyes. Every moment your eyes are open, these neurons flash pictures to your brain.

Deep inside your ear, well past your ear drum, are about 16,000 neurons that carry sound messages to your brain. These neurons allow you to hear everything from a soft whisper to the roar of a jet plane.

Inside your nose, way up at the top, are about five million special neurons that send smell reports to your brain. Scientists say that most people can recognize up to 10,000 separate odors.

Your tongue is covered with neurons called taste buds. Taste buds report sweet, sour, salty, and bitter tastes to your brain. You have about 10,000 taste buds in all.

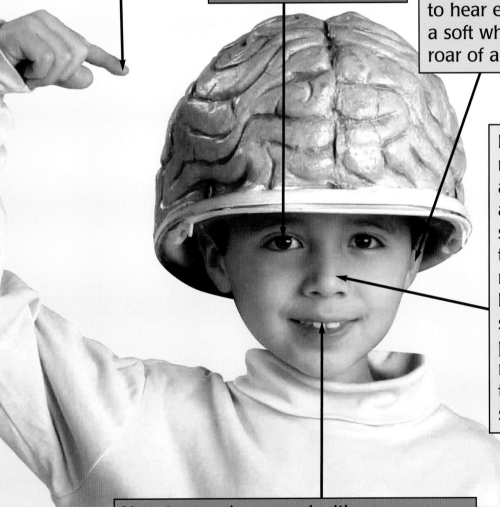

MAKING SENSE OF SENSES

HERE ARE SOME FUN ACTIVITIES THAT WILL HELP YOU LEARN MORE ABOUT YOUR SENSES.

SIGHT

At the back of your eye is the **retina**. The retina is like a movie screen made up of about one hundred million neurons. When light reaches these neurons, they send information to the brain. There is a place on the retina that is called your "blind spot." This is a spot that does not have neurons. To help you find your blind spot, try this:

Hold the page of this book about 20 inches (50 cm) away from your face. Close your right eye. Look at the + with your left eye. Slowly bring the page closer while you look at the +. At a certain distance, the dot will disappear from sight. This is where the dot hits your blind spot.

●   +

SQUIRT says...
A LOT OF USEFUL INFORMATION COMES FROM MORE THAN ONE SENSE AT A TIME. EVEN IN THE DARK, YOUR SENSES OF TASTE, TOUCH, AND SMELL CAN HELP YOUR BRAIN IDENTIFY A LEMON SLICE!

HEARING

Close your eyes and listen carefully for one minute. How many different sounds were you able to hear? Write them down. Try this activity at different times during the day and see how the sounds change.

SMELL

Close your eyes and ask your parents to hold different foods under your nose. See how many you can identify by smell alone.

TASTE

You cannot taste anything if it is not wet with saliva. The saliva allows chemicals in the food to **dissolve** onto your tongue. Dry your tongue well on a clean paper towel or napkin. When your tongue is dry, put a little salt on it. Can you taste the salt?

TOUCH

With the help of a parent, take a walk around your house with your eyes closed tight. Move slowly and touch objects as you go. See if you can name the object you touch. Try this activity again, but this time touch the objects with your elbow. Does this make a difference?

THE LOVE OF LEARNING

I LOVE TO LEARN. LEARNING IS MY FAVORITE PASTIME. I LEARN BY READING, BY LISTENING, AND BY ASKING QUESTIONS. I LEARN ALL THE TIME AND IN ALL KINDS OF WAYS.

BRAIN POWER

Your brain is not a muscle, but it grows more powerful each time you learn something new. There are all kinds of ways to give your brain a good workout.

For example, you can:

Play music

Do puzzles

Play games

Study a new language

Paint a picture

Write a story

FLEX & STRUT say... EVEN THOUGH YOUR BRAIN IS WELL PROTECTED BY THE SKULL BONES, IT CAN STILL GET HURT IF YOU ARE IN A BAD ACCIDENT.

BRAIN PAIN

Keep your brain safe. Here is how:

1. Always wear a helmet when riding your bike, skateboarding, skating, skiing, rollerblading, and snowboarding.

2. Always wear a seat belt in the car.

REST IS BEST

Make sure you get plenty of sleep. Sleep gives your brain a chance to rest a bit. It also allows your brain to sort out and store information it received during the day. Most kids between the ages of 6 and 9 years old need about ten hours of sleep each night. Kids ages 10–12 need a little over nine hours.

BRAIN BELIEFS

I DO NOT MEAN TO BRAG, BUT I AM A FASCINATING ORGAN. FOR THOUSANDS OF YEARS, PEOPLE HAVE BEEN TRYING TO FIGURE OUT HOW I WORK. EVERY DAY, SCIENTISTS DISCOVER MORE AND MORE, BUT I DO NOT THINK THEY WILL EVER FIGURE ME ALL OUT.

PICTURES FROM EGYPT

The ancient Egyptians thought the heart was much more important than the brain. When they created a mummy, the heart was saved, but the brain was thrown away.

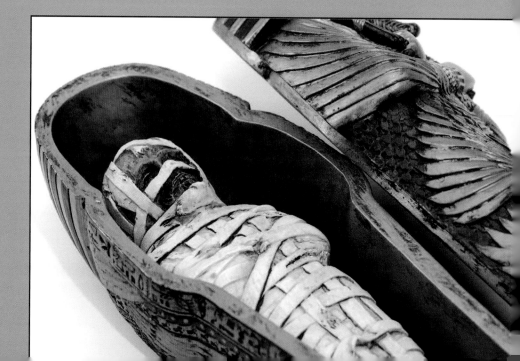

SPECIAL WRITING

The ancient Egyptians had a different form of writing than we do. It used pictures. These pictures were called hieroglyphs. Here is the ancient Egyptian hieroglyph for the word "brain":

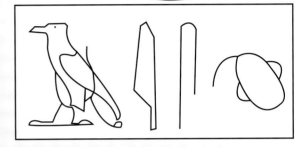

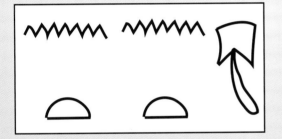

Here is a hieroglyph for the word "meninges" (one of the protective layers around the brain).

BRAIN WAVE

In 1929, a scientist named Hans Berger created an instrument that measures the electrical activity of the brain. This activity is sometimes called brain waves. Here is how brain waves look when they are recorded onto paper.

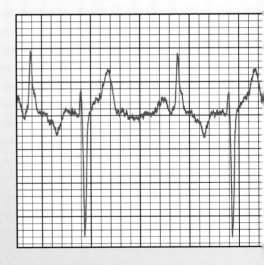

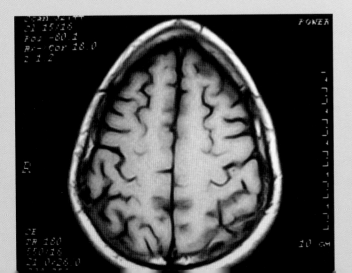

PICTURE THIS

Today, we have special machines that can take computer pictures of the brain. Here is one of them.

FABULOUS PHRASES

BEFORE YOU GO I WANT TO PLAY A GAME. IN THE BOX BELOW YOU WILL SEE SEVEN SENTENCES. EACH SENTENCE HAS THE WORD "NERVE" IN IT. I WILL START A SENTENCE AND YOU TRY TO FILL IN THE BLANK, USING ONE OF THE PHRASES BELOW. FOR EXAMPLE, IF SENTENCE NUMBER 1 IS: "IF SOMEONE GETS SCARED, YOU MIGHT SAY _____." YOU WOULD CHOOSE THE PHRASE "A": "HE LOST HIS NERVE." GOT IT?

Remember, choose a phrase that completes the sentence. The correct matches of sentences and phrases are at the bottom of the page. But you will have to turn the book upside down to read them!

1. If someone gets scared, you might say, _____.

2. If someone does something brave, you might say, _____.

3. If someone says something that makes you angry, you might say, _____.

4. If someone is really upset, you might say, _____.

5. If someone says something mean, you might say, _____.

6. If someone is really bothering you, you might say, _____.

7. If an experience was really frightening, you might say, _____

A. He lost his nerve.

B. She is a bundle of nerves.

C. He really gets on my nerves.

D. That was nerve-racking.

E. You have some nerve.

F. That took a lot of nerve.

G. He touched a nerve.

ANSWERS: 1-A, 2-F, 3-G, 4-B, 5-E, 6-C, 7-D

Amazing Facts About Your Nervous System

BY THE AGE OF TWO YEARS OLD, THE BRAIN IS ABOUT 80% OF THE ADULT SIZE.

THERE ARE APPROXIMATELY ONE QUADRILLION SYNAPSES IN THE HUMAN BRAIN.

THE WORD CEREBELLUM COMES FROM A LATIN WORD THAT MEANS "LITTLE CEREBRUM."

WHEN BABIES ARE BORN, THEY HAVE ALMOST ALL THE NEURONS THEY WILL EVER HAVE.

THE HUMAN BRAIN HAS ABOUT 100,000,000,000 (100 BILLION) NEURONS.

THE BRAIN GROWS AT AN AMAZING RATE BEFORE A BABY IS BORN. AT TIMES 250,000 NEURONS ARE ADDED EVERY MINUTE!

IN HUMANS, THE BRAIN USES 15-20% OF THE BODY'S OXYGEN SUPPLY.

MESSAGES CAN TRAVEL IN NEURONS AT SPEEDS UP TO 268 MILES PER HOUR. (432.29 KM PER HOUR)

THERE ARE ABOUT ONE BILLION NEURONS IN THE HUMAN SPINAL CORD.

A SINGLE NEURON IN YOUR FINGERTIP HAS AN AXON THAT EXTENDS THE LENGTH OF YOUR ARM.

A 75 YEAR OLD PERSON HAS SPENT ABOUT 25 YEARS ASLEEP.

GLOSSARY

coordination The working together of things in a smooth way. The coordination of muscles in the body allows walking, talking, and other activities to take place

dissolve To mix a solid substance, such as sugar or salt, into a liquid so that the substance becomes part of the liquid or evenly spread throughout the liquid

gyri Bulges or raised areas in the cerebral cortex

hemisphere One of two halves of an object that is round or circular. The cerebrum and cerebellum each has two hemispheres

index finger The finger that is next to the thumb

lobes Parts or sections of something, either divided into segments, like the lobes of the brain, or hanging, like earlobes

meninges The protective layers between the brain and the skull

nerves Bands of tissue, usually long and stringy, that carry messages back and forth between the brain and the body's other organs. As a group, the nerves make up the body's nervous system

retina The lining of the back of the eye. The retina contains about 100 million nerve cells that detect images in the form of light entering the eye. These images are then sent to the brain as signals that travel through the optic nerve

sulci Grooves or recessed areas in the cerebral cortex

FOR MORE INFORMATION

BOOKS

Brain Box: The Brain, Nervous System and Senses (Bodyscope). Patricia Macnair. Kingfisher Books Ltd.

The Brain and Nervous System (The Human Machine). Richard Spilsbury. Heinemann.

The Brain: Our Nervous System. Seymour Simon. Collins.

The Nervous System (Body Systems). Susan Heinrichs Gray. Child's World.

The Nervous System (Early Bird Body Systems). Joelle Riley. Lerner Publishing Group.

The Nervous System (True Books). Christine Taylor-Butler. Children's Press.

WEBSITES

Kids Health for Kids

kidshealth.org/kid/htbw/brain.html
Check out this website for in-depth information on your brain and nervous system.

Neuroscience For Kids

faculty.washington.edu/chudler/neurok.html
This website is filled with experiments, activities, and games designed for all students and teachers who would like to discover more about the brain, spinal cord, neurons, and the senses.

Slim Goodbody

www.slimgoodbody.com
Discover loads of fun and free downloads for kids, teachers, and parents.

University of Washington Television

www.uwtv.org/programs/displayevent.aspx?rID=4909
Watch a 30-minute TV show about the nervous system! Five kids along with host Eric Chudler take viewers on an amazing educational journey.

INDEX

Axon 16, 17, 29

Backbone 15
blind spot 22
blood 5, 14
blood vessels 5
bones 4, 5, 6, 7, 15
brain 4, 5, 23, 27
  injury to 25
  messages to
    and from
    9, 15, 17, 21
  parts of 8, 9, 10,
    11, 12, 13, 14,
    15, 19
  pictures of 27
  protecting and
    taking care of
    6, 7, 24–25, 27
  size of 9, 29
brain stem 8, 14–15
brain waves 27
breathing 5, 21

Cells 6, 16, 17
cerebellum 8, 12,
  13, 14, 29
cerebral cortex 9, 11
cerebrospinal fluid 7
cerebrum 8, 9, 10–11,
  12, 13, 14, 20, 29

circulatory system
  4, 5
coordination of
  movement 13
corpus callosum 10

Dendrites 16, 17
digestion and digestive
  system 4, 5, 14

Endocrine system 4
energy 5

Glands 4, 5
gyri 11

Heart 4, 5, 8, 14,
  26, 27
hemispheres 10,
  11, 13
hieroglyphs 27

Intestines 5, 14

Liver 5
lobes 11
lungs 4, 7, 8, 11

Meninges 7, 27
muscles 4, 5, 12, 13,
  14, 15, 24

Nerve cells (neurons)
  16–17
  see also Neurons

nerves 5, 10, 15, 18–19
  sending and
    receiving messages
    through 9, 17, 29
nervous system 4, 5,
  18–19
neurons (nerve cells)
  16–17, 22, 29
  number of 27, 29
  parts of 26, 27
  sensory 17

Organs 6, 8, 11, 26, 27
oxygen 14, 29

Respiratory system 4, 5
retina 22

Safety 7, 25
senses 20–21, 22–23
skeletal system 5
skull 6, 7, 25
sleep 9, 25, 29
spinal cord 5, 15, 18,
  19, 29
stomach 4, 5, 8, 15
sulci 11
synapses 17

Thinking and learning
  8, 9, 14, 24, 27

Wrinkles 11